Standing firm

2 PETER AND JUDE

by Miguel Núñez

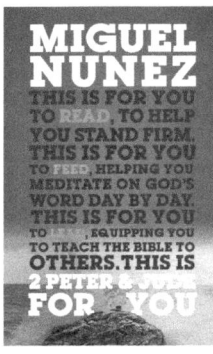

2 Peter and Jude For You

If you are reading *2 Peter and Jude For You* alongside this Good Book Guide, here is how the studies in this booklet link to the chapters of *2 Peter and Jude For You*:

Study One → Ch. 1-2   Study Four → Ch. 5-6
Study Two → Ch. 2-3   Study Five → Ch. 7-8
Study Three → Ch. 4   Study Six → Ch. 8-9

Find out more about *2 Peter and Jude For You* at:
www.thegoodbook.com/for-you
www.thegoodbook.co.uk/for-you

Standing firm
The Good Book Guide to 2 Peter and Jude
© Miguel Núñez/The Good Book Company, 2022.
Series Consultants: Tim Chester, Tim Thornborough,
　　　　　　　　　 Anne Woodcock, Carl Laferton

Published by:
The Good Book Company

thegoodbook.com | thegoodbook.co.uk
thegoodbook.com.au | thegoodbook.co.nz | thegoodbook.co.in

Unless indicated, all Scripture references are taken from The Holy Bible, New International Version, copyright © 2011 Biblica. Used by permission.

Miguel Núñez has asserted his right under the Copyright, Designs and Patents Act 1988 to be identified as the author of this work.

All rights reserved. Except as may be permitted by the Copyright Act, no part of this publication may be reproduced in any form or by any means without prior permission from the publisher.

ISBN: 9781784987121 | ASR | Printed in the UK

CONTENTS

Introduction	4
Why study 2 Peter and Jude?	5
1. How to Keep from Stumbling 2 Peter 1:1-15	7
2. Danger and Judgment 2 Peter 1:16 – 2:10a	13
3. Don't Wander Off 2 Peter 2:10b-22	19
4. How to Wait for the Second Coming 2 Peter 3:1-18	25
5. Fight for the Faith Jude v 1-11	31
6. Glorious Mercy Jude v 12-25	37
Leader's Guide	43

Introduction: Good Book Guides

Every Bible-study group is different—yours may take place in a church building, in a home or in a cafe, on a train, over a leisurely mid-morning coffee or squashed into a 30-minute lunch break. Your group may include new Christians, mature Christians, non-Christians, moms and tots, students, businessmen or teens. That's why we've designed these *Good Book Guides* to be flexible for use in many different situations.

Our aim in each session is to uncover the meaning of a passage, and see how it fits into the "big picture" of the Bible. But that can never be the end. We also need to appropriately apply what we have discovered to our lives. Let's take a look at what is included:

Talkabout: Most groups need to "break the ice" at the beginning of a session, and here's the question that will do that. It's designed to get people talking around a subject that will be covered in the course of the Bible study.

Investigate: The Bible text for each session is broken up into manageable chunks, with questions that aim to help you understand what the passage is about. The **Leader's Guide** contains **guidance for questions**, and sometimes additional "follow-up" questions.

Explore more (optional): These questions will help you connect what you have learned to other parts of the Bible, so you can begin to fit it all together like a jig-saw; or occasionally look at a part of the passage that's not dealt with in detail in the main study.

Apply: As you go through a Bible study, you'll keep coming across **apply** sections. These are questions to get the group discussing what the Bible teaching means in practice for you and your church. **Getting personal** is an opportunity for you to think, plan and pray about the changes that you personally may need to make as a result of what you have learned.

Pray: We want to encourage prayer that is rooted in God's word—in line with his concerns, purposes and promises. So each session ends with an opportunity to review the truths and challenges highlighted by the Bible study, and turn them into prayers of request and thanksgiving.

The **Leader's Guide** and introduction provide historical background information, explanations of the Bible texts for each session, ideas for **optional extra** activities, and guidance on how best to help people uncover the truths of God's word.

Why study 2 Peter and Jude?

Over recent years we have witnessed the fall of a significant number of Christian leaders. Many of these leaders were running well at some point in their lives, but then they stumbled and fell into serious sin. And this is something that could happen to any one of us—church leaders and church members alike—however well we are running today.

Peter and Jude, two leaders in the early church, knew that firsthand. The brothers and sisters they were writing to had fallen under the influence of false teachers who were sexually immoral, financially greedy and power-hungry. A terrible combination! The danger was that through the wrong teaching and immoral example of these leaders, the believers would fall away from faith themselves.

In the two letters we will study in this guide, Peter and Jude both show a deep concern and an intense sense of urgency about the future of the believing communities they are addressing. They write to help their readers to stand firm. Their words are as relevant today as they were in the 1st century.

When it comes to our Christian walk, remaining on track is, on one level, the responsibility of each one of us. Peter says, "Make every effort to confirm your calling and election. For if you do these things, you will never stumble" (2 Peter 1:10). But at another level, finishing well is the work of God. Jude acknowledges that God is the one, in the end, who can keep us from stumbling (Jude v 24). It is through pursuing him and throwing ourselves on his mercy that we will make it to the end of the race—to be presented before his glorious throne "without fault and with great joy" (v 24).

It is important, as you begin, to approach these letters as being fully inspired by God, which makes them inerrant and infallible; to pray for illumination of your understanding; to adopt a humble and teachable attitude; and to decide to obey their content. God will then bless your study of his word.

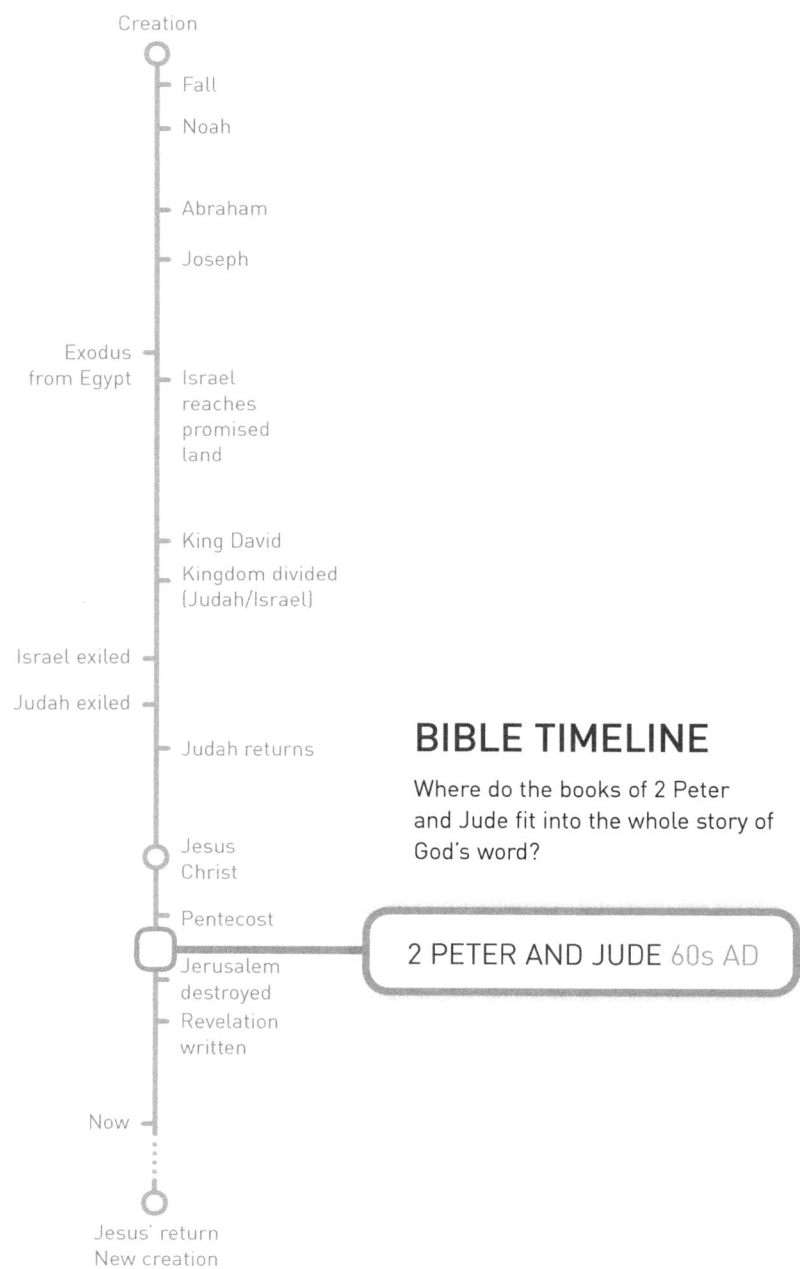

1
2 Peter 1:1-15
HOW TO KEEP FROM STUMBLING

⊕ talkabout

1. What do you think it means to stand firm—or not stand firm—as a Christian?

⊙ investigate

> **Read 2 Peter 1:1-15**

2. Look at Peter's opening greetings (v 1-2). What has enabled his readers to gain faith, grace, and peace?

> **DICTIONARY**
> **Apostle (v 1):** one of those directly appointed by the risen Christ to teach about him.
> **Corruption (v 4):** decay.
> **In increasing measure (v 8):** more and more.

3. God hasn't just saved us—what else has he made possible, and how (v 3-4)?

4. How do verses 3-4 motivate us to pursue godliness?

⊡ explore more

Hebrews 11 gives examples of Old Testament heroes who trusted in the promises of God and, as a result, did not waver in their faith.

▶ Read Hebrews 11:8-10, 17-19

What promise did Abraham receive (v 8)?

What did that lead him to do (v 9)?

What else was Abraham able to do because of trusting God's promises (v 17-19)?

What do you admire about this type of faith?

5. Peter's readers have faith already. But what else does he want them to have (v 5-7)? What does each of these things mean, do you think?

- Why is it important to pursue those things (v 8)?

⇒ apply

6. Practically, what will be the effect of these virtues?

⊡ getting personal

Meditate on where you are regarding the virtues mentioned by Peter in verses 5-7. What are some areas for growth? What would be some signs that you had grown in those areas?

⬇ investigate

7. If someone doesn't pursue godliness, what does that imply about them (v 9)?

8. In what sense do you think that living a godly life serves to "confirm" the fact that we've been called and chosen by God (v 10)?

- What will be the end result of having been called by God and having lived a godly life (v 11)?

9. Why is Peter so determined to write this letter now (v 12-15)?

- Which words and phrases express this determination and sense of urgency?

10. Peter's readers know the truth—so why do you think he wants to remind them of it?

11. In today's passage as a whole, what's the relationship between knowledge of God and godly living?

- How would you sum up what God does and what we are called to do?

⊡ getting personal

Some people are so confident in God's forgiveness that they end up not making much effort to fight sin. Some try desperately to be perfect on their own, fearing that they are not really saved. Which do you tend toward? How does this passage challenge or encourage you?

⊖ apply

12. What steps can you take to remind yourself of the truth? How will this help you to stand firm in your faith?

- What is one thing you could do to help someone else stand firm in their faith this week?

⊓ pray

Spend time listing the truths of the gospel and praising God for them. Pray for one another, asking for God's help in standing firm and living fruitful lives for his glory.

2 Peter 1:16 – 2:10a
DANGER AND JUDGMENT

The story so far

Peter began by helping us to see how to run the Christian life well. God has provided everything we need, but it is up to us to use what he has provided.

⊕ talkabout

1. What qualities might someone have that would make others trust their teaching or leadership?

⊙ investigate

> **Read 2 Peter 1:16-21**

2. In verses 16-18, what reasons are there to pay attention to Peter's teaching?

DICTIONARY

Devised (v 16): invented.
The Majestic Glory (v 17): God.
Sacred (v 18): holy.
The prophetic message (v 19): the Old Testament.
Prophecy (v 20): message from God.
Prophet (v 21): someone who spoke on God's behalf.

The Good Book Guide to 2 Peter and Jude | 13

3. Peter also wants us to pay attention to the rest of Scripture ("the prophetic message"). What is it like (v 19)?

4. What makes it reliable (v 20-21)?

☐ **getting personal**

Imagine an airplane pilot waiting for lights to appear on a dark runway. He or she needs the light in order to land in the right place. In our lives, we do have the light we need to land: the testimony of God's word. But if we ignore it, we will crash!

In our day the individual's viewpoint is often seen as the most important source of truth. In what ways might you be at risk of falling into that way of thinking? How can you make sure that God's word is the light you live by?

5. Look ahead to 2:1-3. What danger is facing Peter's readers? How will what he has written in 1:16-21 help them to face it?

⇒ apply

6. What might hold people back from reading or believing the Bible? How does what we have read so far motivate you to love and listen to God's word?

⬇ investigate

▶ **Read 2 Peter 2:1-10a**

7. What makes the false teachers hard to spot—and why is that so dangerous (2:1)?

DICTIONARY
Heresies (v 1): lies about God.
Sovereign (v 1): ruling over all.
Depraved (v 2): wicked.
Disrepute (v 2): a bad reputation.
Fabricated (v 3): made up.

- What are the possible effects of their teaching on others (v 2-3)?

These false teachers seem to have identified themselves as Christians; in the eyes of others and perhaps even in their own eyes, they had been bought by the Lord (v 1). But by living a lie and not accepting Jesus' lordship, they made it clear that they never really belonged to the family of God.

8. What is going to happen to these false teachers (v 3)?

9. Peter appeals to three examples (v 4-9). What two things do these examples prove (v 9)?

10. How do we see these things in each example?
- Angels (v 4):

Note: This verse may seem strange. We don't often talk about God judging angels. Many scholars believe that this refers to the fall of Satan, who began as an angelic being but rebelled against God. It could also link to 1 Peter 3:19-20, which some interpret as a reference to angels who sinned in the days of Noah. But regardless of who exactly these "spirits" were and what they had done, the main point is to understand what God's response was to their sin.

- The flood (2 Peter 2:5; see Genesis 7:10 – 8:22):

- Sodom and Gomorrah (2 Peter 2:6-8; see Genesis 18:20 – 19:29):

ⓘ explore more

optional

The example of Lot as a godly man is interesting given Lot's track record. Lot lived in Sodom, which was renowned as a city of immorality.

What consequences did this have for Lot (2 Peter 2:7-8)?

▶ **Read Genesis 19:1-8**

Do you think Lot acted righteously in this case?

God showed mercy to Lot, rescuing him from Sodom when he destroyed it (v 15-16). This should encourage us: sinners can be objects of God's redeeming and unmerited favor—though we should not see this as a license to sin.

11. What do you think Peter means by "follow[ing] the corrupt desire of the flesh" and "despis[ing] authority" (2 Peter 2:10)? (Look back at verses 1-3 to see some examples of how the false teachers were doing this.)

⇥ apply

12. What particular teachings might tempt us to "despise [the] authority" of Jesus and Scripture today?

- Practically, how can we keep ourselves in the truth?

⊡ getting personal

How do you respond to these stories? Which is the greater motivation for you to pursue godliness and truth—the fact that God rescues his people or the judgment that is coming to the unrighteous? How can you use either or both motivations to keep reminding yourself to pursue God's way?

⊡ pray

Use Psalm 119 to praise God for his word and commit yourselves to following it. This long psalm is divided into sections, each of eight verses. Each person could choose their own section, so that everyone prays on the basis of different verses. Or you could read a few sections together.

3 2 Peter 2:10b-22
DON'T WANDER OFF

The story so far

Peter began by helping us to see how to run the Christian life well. God has provided everything we need, but it is up to us to use what he has provided.

This means we must remember what we know about God. Peter explained that his teachings came from God and warned against listening to false teachers.

⊕ talkabout

1. What's the link between the things we believe and the way we behave? Can you think of examples where someone's beliefs have led them to act in particular ways?

⊕ investigate

> **Read 2 Peter 2:10b-22**

2. Peter has said that the false teachers "despise authority." Why do they do that—what is their view of themselves (v 10)?

> **DICTIONARY**
>
> **Celestial (v 10):** in the heavens.
> **Blaspheme (v 12):** speak in a way that is offensive to God.
> **Unreasoning (v 12):** irrational.
> **Carouse (v 13):** this word probably refers to wild drinking parties.
> **Blemishes (v 13):** stains.
> **Revelling (v 13):** enjoying oneself.
> **Brood (v 14):** group of offspring.

• But what is Peter's view of them (v 12)?

3. What particular actions reveal their misguided arrogance (v 10-12)?

Note: "Celestial beings"—Peter seems to be referring here to angels who have fallen. They are going to be judged by God (see verse 4). Other angels are stronger than these fallen celestial beings and are able to bring God's judgment upon them; but it is God's judgment, not theirs.

4. What lifestyle do the false teachers live (v 13-14)?

• But what is Peter's view of them (v 12)?

5. What impact have they had…

• on others (v 13, 14, 18)?

• on themselves (v 20)?

⇥ apply

6. Who or what promises "freedom" today? What are they really offering people?

⊡ getting personal

Who do you know who may be particularly vulnerable to temptation—perhaps because their faith is "unstable" (v 14) or because they have only just become Christians (v 18)? What could you do to support and encourage these individuals in their faith?

⊡ explore more

Verses 15-16 compare the false teachers of Peter's day with Balaam, an Old Testament prophet whose story we read in Numbers 22 – 25. Balaam was offered a bribe by the king of the Moabites to declare a curse on Israel. At first he refused, but then he ended up going with the king's messengers. He was tempted to disobey God and curse God's people because he "loved the wages of wickedness" (2 Peter 2:15).

▶ **Read Numbers 22:21-35**

Why does the angel of the LORD stop Balaam?

What's the contrast between Balaam and the donkey?

In 2 Peter 2:15, how does Peter highlight Balaam's sinfulness?

Like Balaam, the false teachers were greedy, immoral men who loved money more than God. They knew the way of truth, but they decided to leave it and renounce the faith.

⬇ investigate

7. Peter says that the false teachers "left the straight way and wandered off" (v 15). In verses 20-21, how else does he describe what has happened?

• Verse 22 compares the false teachers to a dog returning to its vomit and a sow returning to the mud. What have the false teachers returned to?

8. Why is what they have done so serious (v 20-21)?

9. How do you think this happened? What might the first steps have been?

10. What's the end result of taking this path? Look back through the passage and find all the times Peter highlights the false teachers' ultimate destiny.

11. Look back at 2 Peter 1. What does Peter want his readers to do, in order to avoid becoming like the false teachers?

⊡ getting personal

What sins here do you recognise as tempting for yourself? You may not have committed adultery, but are you tempted by lust? You may not be exploiting people, but do you think too much about money? Think about what truths about God you could keep in mind to help you live a godly life. Ask God to keep on driving you toward the light in whatever area is most tempting for you.

⊖ apply

12. When we are tempted to sin, what should we do?

⊕ pray

In Ephesians 6, Paul encourages us to "stand firm then, with the belt of truth buckled around your waist" (v 14) and to wield "the sword of the Spirit, which is the word of God" (v 17). God's truth is the key to our fight against the world, the flesh, and the devil. Jesus has already defeated evil, and so we can be confident that with his help, we can win this battle. Pray for one another now, that you may put Paul's instructions into practice and that God will enable you to stand firm against the devil's lies.

4
2 Peter 3:1-18
HOW TO WAIT FOR THE SECOND COMING

The story so far

Peter began by helping us to see how to run the Christian life well. God has provided everything we need, but it is up to us to use what he has provided.

This means we must remember what we know about God. Peter explained that his teachings came from God and warned against listening to false teachers.

False teachers have "wandered off" from the right path, despite knowing the truth—and they entice others away. Peter's strong language is a warning to us.

⇄ talkabout
1. What is your understanding of what will happen when Jesus returns?

⬇ investigate
> **Read 2 Peter 3:1-18**

2. Peter starts by reminding us of the purpose of his letter. What does he want his readers to do (v 1-2)?

DICTIONARY
Deluged (v 6): flooded.
Reserved (v 7): set aside, kept.
Repentance (v 9): turning away from sin.
The day of the Lord (v 10): the day when Jesus comes back.
Elements (v 10): the fundamental building blocks of the world.
Salvation (v 15): being saved.
Paul (v 15): the writer of a number of New Testament letters.
The lawless (v 17): those who do not follow God's law.

3. He specifically wants us to believe in the second coming of the Lord Jesus. What does he say will happen on that day (v 7)?

4. Some people say this won't happen. Why (v 3-4)?

5. Peter reminds us of the flood in order to counter the false teachers' argument (v 5-7). Why? What connections are there between the flood and the second coming?

6. How does Peter explain why God seems to be slow in keeping his promise (v 8-9)?

⮕ apply

7. If we are looking forward to the second coming of Jesus, what should our attitude be now toward wickedness and ungodly people?

⊡ getting personal

How do you feel about Christ's return? Do you hope, deep down, that he won't come yet, because there are things you want to do or experience in this world first? How can you make sure you wait with joyful expectation?

⊡ investigate

8. What will the day of the Lord be like (v 10)?

9. How should this motivate us to live (v 11-14)?

- Why?

As Peter said in verse 9, the reason Christ has not returned yet is because he will save many more before he does. Paul also spoke about this (v 15-16). But it seems some were saying that God's patience means it doesn't matter how much someone sins.

10. What does Peter think about this interpretation of Paul's teaching (v 16)?

- How do you think Peter would counter their argument? (Look back at 1:19-21; 2:4-10; and 3:5-7.)

explore more

We can see in Paul's letters his own frustration at this distortion of his teaching. His letter to the Romans helps us to get the right understanding. We are saved only by God's grace and not by our own goodness. At the same time, we are also called to pursue goodness with all our strength.

▶ Read Romans 6:1-2

Why are some people saying we should keep on sinning (v 1)?

But why does this make no sense (v 2)?

Paul unpacks this more in the following verses. Because Jesus died and rose again, it's as if we have also died and risen again to new life. This means that instead of having sin as our master, we now have God. We have "been set free from sin and have become slaves to righteousness" (v 18). In other words, Christians pursue righteousness because that is our new identity.

▶ Read Romans 6:22-23

How do we gain eternal life?

How could we use Paul's words to answer someone who says, "If you're forgiven, you can just sin as much as you want"?

⇨ apply

11. Why is it so important to "be on your guard" (2 Peter 3:17) about what you believe about the second coming in particular?

12. Peter calls us to grow in grace (which means growing to be like Jesus) and in the knowledge of God (v 18). How can you seek this kind of growth this week?

⋯ getting personal

If we want to know what a Christian who has grown in grace looks like, we only need to read Galatians 5:22-23: "But the fruit of the Spirit is love, joy, peace, forbearance, kindness, goodness, faithfulness, gentleness and self-control." Ask yourself how much you display these qualities. Choose one or two and ask for God's help in growing you in grace in this area.

⇧ pray

"To him be glory both now and forever!" (2 Peter 3:18).

Spend some time praising God. Start with what you have learned in this letter but feel free to praise him for any other aspects of his character too.

5 Jude v 1-11
FIGHT FOR THE FAITH

The story so far

2 Peter was written to help us run the Christian life well. We must stick to the truth rather than listening to destructive false teachings.

Peter concluded by looking to the day of judgment, when evil will be destroyed and righteousness will reign. Looking forward to this means living godly lives.

⊕ talkabout

1. "It's worth fighting for." What might we say that about?

⊡ investigate

▶ **Read Jude v 1-11**

2. What three privileges of Christians does Jude highlight in verse 1?

- What three blessings does he pray for his readers in verse 2?

DICTIONARY

Contend (v 3): fight.
Pervert (v 4): distort; change in a wrong way.
Delivered (v 5): saved; brought out of.
Proper (v 6): suitable, correct.
The great Day (v 6): the day when Jesus comes back.
Perversion (v 7): distortion.
Archangel (v 9): a leader among the angels.
Disputing (v 9): arguing, battling.
Slander (v 9): telling lies about someone.
Rebuke (v 9): tell off.
Woe (v 11): sorrow, distress.

3. Why does Jude feel "compelled" to write (v 3)? What has happened?

> Jude's opponents "pervert[ed] the grace of our God into a license for immorality." In other words, they claimed that believers could live as they wished, counting on God's grace to forgive them in the future. But God did not give us his grace to encourage us to sin freely; he gave it to empower us to obey all of his commandments.

4. Jude wants his readers to "contend" (or fight) for the faith.

   - Why do you think it is important that this faith has been entrusted to them "once for all" (v 3)?

   - Why do you think Jude describes faith as something to be fought for?

5. Taking into account both verse 1 and verses 3-4, what does it mean to have faith in Jesus?

⟹ apply

6. What does it look like to uphold Jesus as "our only Sovereign and Lord" (v 3)?

getting personal

Bible commentator David Helm writes, "On your feet. The time for leisure is past. Contend. Agonize. Exert maximum effort. The Christian faith, in all its fullness and completeness, is worthy of your struggle" (*1 & 2 Peter and Jude*, p 297). How seriously do you take your faith? What step could you take to contend for it more seriously?

investigate

7. In the examples in verses 5-7, what did God do, and why?

- v 5

- v 6

- v 7

- Why do you think Jude wants to remind his readers of these things?

8. What are the "ungodly people" of Jude's day doing, and on what basis (v 8)?

Jude now tells us that the archangel Michael did not dare to pronounce judgment against the devil but deferred to God's authority. He left the judgment to God. But the false teachers are acting as if they have authority over celestial beings. Jude compares them to irrational animals. They know by instinct that there are celestial beings, but they do not know how to properly behave toward them.

⊡ explore more

There is no other biblical reference to the event described in verse 9. However, in Jewish literature, there is a book called *The Assumption of Moses*, which many early Christians knew and believed. (This doesn't mean we should accept everything in that book as true; we can trust only that the books in the canon of Scripture are inspired by God. As one of the writers of Scripture, Jude had special insight, and so we can trust that this particular example is true.) Here, we're told that the archangel Michael is the one who buried Moses. Satan tried to steal Moses' body, and Michael said, "May the Lord rebuke you."

How does this show respect for God's authority?

There are several other references to Michael in the Bible. In Daniel, he is described as a "prince" who protects Israel (10:13, 21; 12:1). In Revelation 12:7, he battles against the dragon, which represents Satan.

▶ **Read Revelation 12:7-10**

How is God's authority made clear here?

Jude v 11 compares the false teachers with three more examples of sin which has been judged by God. Cain rebelled against God by becoming angry when God rejected his offering (Genesis 4:1-5). Balaam was tempted to curse God's people for money (Numbers 22). Korah rebelled against the authority of Moses and Aaron (Numbers 16).

9. How do these examples match what the false teachers of Jude's own day are doing? Think especially about...

- their attitude toward God's authority.

- their motivation.

- their final destiny.

10. What do all Jude's examples tell us about how and why people might fall into sin?

getting personal

Do you recognize any of these tendencies in yourself? Pause to consider whether you could be in danger of falling into any of these traps, and to ask God for his help. Remember, he is the one who has called you, loves you, and keeps you for Jesus Christ (Jude v 1).

11. Based on what we have read so far, how would you sum up…

• what it means to sin?

• God's attitude toward sin?

• the attitude we ought to have toward God?

➔ apply

12. Imagine you realized that a fellow believer was being tempted toward sin. How could you follow Jude's example and help them to contend for their faith?

⬆ pray

Write down a list of different areas of life (for example, work, family, home, leisure). Together, offer each one up to God, asking him to help you recognize his authority over everything you do. Confess where you are living your own way instead of his. Thank him for his grace to you in Christ.

6 Jude v 12-25
GLORIOUS MERCY

The story so far

Jude began his letter by encouraging us to fight for the faith. God has given us knowledge of him. We must respond by upholding his authority in every area.

talkabout

1. When you see someone doing something wrong, what do you tend to do?

investigate

> **Read Jude v 12-25**

Jude has been comparing the false teachers of his time with Old Testament figures. Now he continues to describe their wickedness.

2. What do the images in verses 12-13 show about…

 • the false teachers' impact on Jude's readers?

DICTIONARY
Blemishes (v 12): this word can also be translated "hidden reefs."
Qualm (v 12): hesitation.
Foretold (v 17): predicted.
The last times (v 18): the times we are in now, after Jesus ascended to heaven and until he comes again.
Corrupted (v 23): sinful. Literally, decayed.

- their character?

- their ultimate destiny?

In verses 14-15, Jude cites a book called Enoch. This is not part of the Bible. However, Jude does want us to listen to its words—at least the ones he quotes here. (We shouldn't consider it strange that Jude quotes from a book that is not part of Scripture. Other Bible books do the same thing—for example, Acts 17:23, 28.) God inspired Jude to know that this information was reliable and important to communicate.

3. What did Enoch say would happen to "ungodly sinners"?

4. What specific examples of the false teachers' sin does Jude list in verse 16?

getting personal

Have you ever refused to help someone because the cost was too much? If so, admit this to God and ask him to help you to do better next time. Is there a friend, neighbor, or family member you could help this week, no matter what it costs you?

5. How does Jude help us to understand why these people are acting in the way they do (v 17-19)?

6. Jude's condemnation of sin is very severe. But how does he show tenderness as he addresses his readers?

- What does he call them to do (v 20)?

⇒ apply

7. How does this give us hope in our own struggles with sin?

- What can we do practically to put Jude's instructions into practice?

⊡ explore more

Jude also instructs us to keep ourselves in God's love (v 21).

▶ **Read John 15:10 and 1 John 3:24**

What does it mean to keep ourselves in God's love?

⊡ investigate

8. In verses 22-23, how does Jude call us to show the same tenderness toward fellow believers and the same hatred of sin that he has shown?

⊡ apply

9. How can we put these instructions into practice—contending for one another's faith as well as our own?

⊡ getting personal

Which aspect of Jude's writing comes most naturally to you—his tenderness and love or his willingness to be severe in his condemnation of sin? How could you grow in the aspect which comes less naturally to you?

In his closing sentence, Jude turns his masterful use of language away from human sinfulness and toward the glory of the Creator God.

10. What is God able to do for us (v 24)?

11. What do we owe him (v 25)?

⤳ apply

12. How will recognizing these things keep us from stumbling?

- What can we do to keep reminding ourselves of these truths?

⤒ pray

Meditate together on God's glory, majesty, power, and authority. Share things which lead you to praise him—perhaps particular Bible verses, songs, or experiences. Then spend time glorifying him together.

Standing firm
LEADER'S GUIDE

Leader's Guide

INTRODUCTION

Leading a Bible study can be a bit like herding cats—everyone has a different idea of what the passage could be about, and a different line of enquiry that they want to pursue. But a good group leader is more than someone who just referees this kind of discussion. You will want to:

- correctly understand and handle the Bible passage. But also…

- encourage and train the people in your group to do this for themselves. Don't fall into the trap of spoon-feeding people by simply passing on the information in the Leader's Guide. Then…

- make sure that no Bible study is finished without everyone knowing how the passage is relevant for them. What changes do you all need to make in the light of the things you have been learning? And finally…

- encourage the group to turn all that has been learned and discussed into prayer.

Your Bible-study group is unique, and you are likely to know better than anyone the capabilities, backgrounds and circumstances of the people you are leading. That's why we've designed these guides with a number of optional features. If they're a quiet bunch, you might want to spend longer on *talkabout*. If your time is limited, you can choose to skip *explore more*, or get people to look at these questions at home. Can't get enough of Bible study? Well, some studies have optional extra homework projects. As leader, you can adapt and select the material to the needs of your particular group.

So what's in the Leader's Guide? The main thing that this Leader's Guide will help you to do is to understand the major teaching points in the passage you are studying, and how to apply them. As well as guidance for the questions, the Leader's Guide for each session contains the following important sections:

THE BIG IDEA

One or two key sentences will give you the main point of the session. This is what you should be aiming to have fixed in people's minds as they leave the Bible study. And it's the point you need to head back toward when the discussion goes off at a tangent.

SUMMARY

An overview of the passage, including plenty of useful historical background information.

OPTIONAL EXTRA

Usually this is an introductory activity that ties in with the main theme of the Bible study, and is designed to "break the ice" at the beginning of a session. Or it may be a "homework project" that people can tackle during the week.

So let's take a look at the various different features of a Good Book Guide:

⊕ talkabout

Each session kicks off with a discussion question, based on the group's opinions or experiences. It's designed to get people talking and thinking in a general way about the main subject of the Bible study.

⬇ investigate

The first thing you and your group need to know is what the Bible passage is about, which is the purpose of these questions. But watch out—people may come up with answers based on their experiences or teaching they have heard in the past, without referring to the passage at all. It's amazing how often we can get through a Bible study without actually looking at the Bible! If you're stuck for an answer, the Leader's Guide contains guidance for questions. These are the answers to direct your group to. This information isn't meant to be read out to people—ideally, you want them to discover these answers from the Bible for themselves. Sometimes there are optional follow-up questions (see ☒ in guidance for questions) to help you help your group get to the answer.

⊡ explore more

These questions generally point people to other relevant parts of the Bible. They are useful for helping your group to see how the passage fits into the "big picture" of the whole Bible. These sections are OPTIONAL—only use them if you have time. Remember that it's better to finish in good time having really grasped one big thing from the passage, than to try and cram everything in.

⤳ apply

We want to encourage you to spend more time working at application—too often, it is simply tacked on at the end. In the Good Book Guides, apply sections are mixed in with the investigate sections of the study. We hope that people will realize that application is not just an optional extra, but rather, the whole purpose of studying the Bible. We do Bible study so that our lives can be changed by what we hear from God's word. If you skip the application, the Bible study hasn't achieved its purpose.

These questions draw out practical lessons that we can all learn from the Bible passage. You can review what has been learned so far, and think about practical differences that this should make in our churches and our lives. The group gets the opportunity to talk about what they personally have learned.

⊡ getting personal

These can be done at home, but it is well worth allowing a few moments of quiet reflection during the study for each person to think and pray about specific changes they need to make in their own lives. Why not have a time for reporting back at the beginning of the following session, so that everyone can be encouraged and challenged by one another to make application a priority?

⬆ pray

In Acts 4:25-30 the first Christians quoted Psalm 2 as they prayed in response to the persecution of the apostles by the Jewish religious leaders. Today however, it's not as common for Christians to base prayers on the truths of God's word as it once was. As a result, our prayers tend to be weak, superficial and self-centered rather than bold, visionary and God-centered.

The prayer section is based on what has been learned from the Bible passage. How different our prayer times would be if we were genuinely responding to what God has said to us through his word.

1
2 Peter 1:1-15
HOW TO KEEP FROM STUMBLING

THE BIG IDEA
We need to work to keep in mind what we know about God—and then live godly lives in the light of that knowledge. This is how to stand firm as a Christian.

SUMMARY
Peter begins the first chapter of his letter by helping us see how to run the Christian life well. His hope for his readers is in verses 10-11: "If you do these things, you will never stumble, and you will receive a rich welcome into the eternal kingdom of our Lord and Saviour Jesus Christ."

Peter's greetings help us to see that our faith—and the grace and peace that go with it—is received as a result of the knowledge of Jesus and his redeeming work (v 1-2). He follows this with an extraordinary revelation (v 3-4): through this knowledge, we are not only saved from God's wrath but also equipped to live a godly life. God has provided everything we need to live a victorious life to the very end.

But it is up to us to develop and use what he has provided. Peter lists a series of virtues which all Christians should be making "every effort" to grow in (v 5-7). This will confirm the fact that we have indeed been saved (v 8, 10). We must not let our knowledge of God stagnate, or we will end up forgetting what we have gained (v 9).

Peter writes with a great sense of urgency. He himself does not have long left to live, and, as a result, he is doing everything he can to make sure his readers remember the truths they know about God (v 12-15). He wants them not just to finish the race but to finish strong.

OPTIONAL EXTRA
2 Peter 1:3 tells us that God has given us everything we need for a life of godliness. Invite the group to think about what they would need for a journey through the jungle or other wilderness. You could prep some objects (or pictures) beforehand: for example, insect repellent, food, light clothes, a sunhat, walking boots. Think about the jungle scenario: what might happen if you didn't have one of these things? You could also label these objects "knowledge of God," "grace and peace," "faith," "virtue," "self-control," and the other virtues listed in verses 5-7. What might happen in the life of faith if we don't have these things?

GUIDANCE FOR QUESTIONS
1. What do you think it means to stand firm—or not stand firm—as a Christian?
We will see in 2 Peter and Jude that people fall away from the faith in two ways: through false teachings (believing lies about God) and through immoral living. The two are closely linked. So standing firm means both knowing the truth about God and living in the light of that truth. Encourage the group to share their own thoughts and ideas, and to be specific about what it might look like to fall away or to stand firm.

2. Look at Peter's opening greetings

(v 1-2). What has enabled his readers to gain faith, grace, and peace? We have received faith "through the righteousness of our God and Savior Jesus Christ" (v 1). In other words, we have not received faith through our own merits. We have received it as a gift of grace from Jesus Christ, who went to the cross and shed his blood on our behalf. Grace and peace are also received as a result of the redeeming work of Christ (v 2). Without knowledge of him, there is no way to enjoy these blessings. With it, they are ours "in abundance."

3. God hasn't just saved us—what else has he made possible, and how (v 3-4)? We are not only saved from the wrath of God; we are also equipped by grace to live a godly life (v 3). The power to live in a way that honors God is received through knowledge of him (v 3): the more we know God, the more we become like him. God's promises aid us in our walk with him (v 4). They help us endure suffering as we look ahead to what he has promised.

4. How do verses 3-4 motivate us to pursue godliness? These verses show us that godliness really is possible, by God's power at work in us. Therefore, we can pursue it confidently. Peter goes so far as to say that we "participate in the divine nature" as we become more Christ-like. This is a gift well worth pursuing.

EXPLORE MORE
Read Hebrews 11:8-10, 17-19.
What promise did Abraham receive (v 8)? God promised him a land that he would receive as his inheritance.

What did that lead him to do (v 9)? He went and made his home in the promised land, even though he was a stranger there.

What else was Abraham able to do because of trusting God's promises (v 17-19)? He offered his son Isaac as a sacrifice, obeying God's command even though it did not seem to make sense. God had promised him descendants through Isaac, so why would he tell Abraham to kill Isaac? But Abraham was still willing to obey. He trusted in God's power to raise Isaac from the dead if necessary.

What do you admire about this type of faith? Abraham obeyed God even when it must have been deeply tempting not to. His trust in God was rock-solid. But encourage the group to share whatever they personally admire—there's no one right answer here.

5. Peter's readers have faith already. But what else does he want them to have (v 5-7)? What does each of these things mean, do you think?
- Goodness: That is, moral excellence. We will never reach moral perfection this side of eternity, but we can live lives that are not characterized by sin but by righteousness.
- Knowledge: This is not the knowledge of God that leads to salvation (unlike the "knowledge" in verses 2 and 3, where a different Greek word is used). It is a practical wisdom and discernment about how to live well. This type of knowledge does not grow naturally; it is the fruit of living in God's will.
- Self-control: This means having control over our impulses. In order to have self-control, we must be filled with the Spirit.
- Perseverance: This is also translated "patience." It means enduring and being able to stand firm under pressure without giving up our faith.
- Godliness: This refers to a lifestyle that imitates Christ, making every effort to do God's will.

- Mutual affection: This is the concern and love we have for our brothers and sisters, whether they are biological or of our faith family.
- Love: This is *agape*: sacrificial love. This is the kind of love that brought Christ to the cross. It means giving of yourself for the benefit of others.

- **Why is it important to pursue those things (v 8)?** These qualities will "keep [us] from being ineffective and unproductive in [our] knowledge of our Lord Jesus Christ." That is, having these virtues means we are reflecting God's character and bearing fruit.

6. APPLY: Practically, what will be the effect of these virtues? Invite the group to discuss each virtue again. What impact could it have on someone if they are growing in self-control, for example? What will they be like? What will the effect be on others?

7. If someone doesn't pursue godliness, what does that imply about them (v 9)? They have forgotten what Christ has done for them. For this reason, Peter refers to such Christians as being "blind." They have voluntarily chosen to shut their eyes to Christ's light and his work.

8. In what sense do you think that living a godly life serves to "confirm" the fact that we've been called and chosen by God (v 10)? If we turn from sin and seek the qualities Peter has recommended, it is proof that we have indeed been saved and that the Spirit of the Lord is within us.

- **What will be the end result of having been called by God and having lived a godly life (v 11)?** We will one day receive a "rich welcome" before the eternal throne of God.

9. Why is Peter so determined to write this letter now (v 12-15)? In some way, the Lord had revealed to Peter that after writing this letter he would soon be departing his life. This means he wrote with a sense of urgency. He was determined to make sure that his readers would remember the truth, so that they would finish the race of the Christian life and not fall away.

- **Which words and phrases express this determination and sense of urgency?**
  - "always" (v 12)
  - "as long as I live" (v 13)
  - "soon" (v 14)
  - "make every effort" (v 15)
  - "always" (v 15)

10. Peter's readers know the truth—so why do you think he wants to remind them of it? With the passing of time, the truths of the Bible, its wonderful stories and great teachings can seem old and the things of the world can seem to shine brighter. What we once thought was amazing becomes ordinary or routine. And what is ordinary is soon out of our memory. Little by little, we drift away. Peter wants to remind his readers of the truth so that their faith does not grow cold.

11. In today's passage as a whole, what's the relationship between knowledge of God and godly living? Knowing God is what allows us to live godly lives (v 3). If we know God, it should make us fruitful (v 8). As we will see, much of 2 Peter highlights one aspect of our knowledge of God: the fact that God judges sin. If we forget that, we will fall into a sinful lifestyle. If we remember it, we will fear the Lord and pursue godliness.

- **How would you sum up what God does and what we are called to do?**

God has given us everything we need for godliness (v 3). But we are still to "make every effort" to live a godly life (v 5). It is possible to know that Jesus is Lord and yet not act upon that knowledge. The degree to which God works in our lives depends on our degree of obedience to his will.

12. APPLY: What steps can you take to remind yourself of the truth? How will this help you to stand firm in your faith? Ask the group to think very practically about their own lives. Encourage them to see the Bible as the source of truth, not anything else. Reading the stories of what God has done—and particularly what Christ did for us through his life, death, and resurrection—will produce in us sorrow over our sin and gratitude for the cleansing we have received.

- **What is one thing you could do to help someone else stand firm in their faith this week?** This is also something we need to encourage one another in! It might be making an effort to discuss the Sunday sermon with someone after the service, or sending a friend an encouraging Bible verse, or offering to pray with someone who is struggling—anything that will remind them of the truths they have learned.

2 Peter 1:16 – 2:10a
DANGER AND JUDGMENT

THE BIG IDEA
God has given us the truth. So don't pay attention to false teachers, who are doomed to destruction.

SUMMARY
After teaching the need to remember what has been learned, Peter goes on to explain the source of his teachings: he speaks as an eyewitness to events surrounding Jesus Christ (1:16-18). This gives him authority. Next, Peter appeals to the authority of God's revelation in the Scriptures of the Old Testament (v 19-21). This written message is "completely reliable" and is the light we need to live by.

Peter's teachings and those of the Scriptures come straight from God, but there are also teachers who bring lies into the church (2:3). They seem like true believers, but they secretly introduce heresies which lead others astray. These false ideas result in immoral behavior and bring Christianity into disrepute.

These false teachings also lead to destruction. God is not indifferent to the distortion of the truth. Peter provides three examples from the past of how God carried out his judgment on those who sinned (v 4-8), affirming that God both rescues the godly and judges the unrighteous (v 9-10a). He is trying to convince us not to pay attention to the false teachers but to submit to the authority of Jesus, our rescuer.

OPTIONAL EXTRA
If you have space outside, hold a tug of war. Stick a small paper figure at the center of the rope and divide the group into two teams. One team represents false teaching and the other team the truth. As both teams pull, which way will the paper figure go? This is a light-hearted way of introducing the key theme of this passage.

GUIDANCE FOR QUESTIONS
1. What qualities might someone have that would make others trust their teaching or leadership? You might discuss any of the following: practical experience of the thing being taught; expert knowledge and insight; a charismatic or sympathetic personality; direct promises of help; a way with words. This question is designed to get the group warmed up ready to think about why people might have trusted Peter's teaching or listened to the false teachers.

2. In verses 16-18, what reasons are there to pay attention to Peter's teaching? Peter speaks as an eyewitness; his teachings are not the invention of his own imagination. He alludes to what he saw and heard at the Mount of Transfiguration (Matthew 17): Jesus shone with glory and the voice of God the Father was heard from heaven. Peter has heard a direct revelation from God. This gives him the authority to speak and write authoritatively about Jesus.

3. Peter also wants us to pay attention to the rest of Scripture ("the prophetic message"). What is it like (v 19)? Scripture is "completely reliable." It is like a light that shines in the midst of sin ("in a dark place") until a transformation

50 LEADER'S GUIDE | Standing firm

takes place in the heart ("the morning star rises"). Scripture is the light of revelation that tells us about God, reveals our own sin, and restores us to repentance.

4. What makes it reliable (v 20-21)? The prophets of God in the past did not just give their own interpretation of what they had experienced. Nor did they receive an idea from God and then interpret and change it. They only wrote what came to them by inspiration. God is the primary author of the Bible: it is the result of divine will.

5. Look at 2:1-3. What danger is facing Peter's readers? How will what he has written in 1:16-21 help them to face it? Peter warns his readers about false teachers who will lead them away from the truth. What he has written about his own authority and that of the Scriptures should help them to recognize what makes a teaching truly trustworthy. It will also motivate them to pursue the truth, which is like a light in their hearts. This should strengthen them against being seduced by false teaching.

6. APPLY: What might hold people back from reading or believing the Bible? How does what we have read so far motivate you to love and listen to God's word?
- Some doubt that the Bible's teaching is good. They would prefer to live the world's way. But Peter helps us to see that it comes from God and is a light in our hearts.
- Some doubt that Scripture is reliable. They say that the text has been corrupted or that we can't be sure that its stories really happened. But Peter appeals to his own experience as an eyewitness of Jesus' majesty. In Acts 4:20, he says, "We cannot help speaking about what we have seen and heard." Only those who had been true eyewitnesses could be so transformed. We can trust his testimony.
- Some simply find it hard to understand and read the Bible for themselves. But this passage makes it clear that God speaks through his word; he is its author. So even if reading the Bible is hard, it is worthwhile. We should also remember that God has given us preachers and teachers to help us understand the Bible. The faithful preaching of God's word is what shines its light into our hearts. This passage can serve as a motivation to pay attention to good Bible teaching.

7. What makes the false teachers hard to spot—and why is that so dangerous (2:1)? Having arisen within the church rather than outside it, they look like any other believer. They introduce their teaching "secretly." This is dangerous because they are teaching lies about God. People are easily becoming sucked into the wrong beliefs about key issues—denying their Lord, for example. Peter terms these "destructive heresies."

- **What are the possible effects of their teaching on others (v 2-3)?** By encouraging other believers to sin, the false teachers are bringing the way of truth "into disrepute" (v 2). Sinful behavior by Christians causes others to speak poorly about the Christian faith. This is not just bad for non-Christians but for Christians too; those who are led astray may risk falling away altogether and bringing destruction on themselves. Also, these believers are being exploited (v 3). The false teachers may claim to be helping, but they are just lining their own pockets and protecting their own power or reputation.

8. What is going to happen to these false teachers (v 3)? God is not indifferent. He will come in judgment on the false teachers and destroy them.

9. Peter appeals to three examples. What two things do these examples prove (v 9)? God rescues the godly from trials. But he also punishes the unrighteous.

10. How do we see these things in each example?
- **Angels (v 4):** God punished angels who had sinned by putting them in chains ready for judgment.
- **The flood (v 5; see Genesis 7:10 – 8:22):** Peter is seeking to illustrate here both that our holy God is capable of taking extreme measures when dealing with sin and that he acts to save the righteous. God punished the entire world—but he also preserved Noah, along with his wife, his three sons, and his sons' wives.
- **Sodom and Gomorrah (v 6-8; see Genesis 18:20 – 19:29):** God burned these cities to ashes. Peter is demonstrating that God always judges the wicked. Like Noah, Lot is used as an example of a godly and righteous man who lived among wicked people and was rescued when they were destroyed. For more on this story, see the Explore More section below.

EXPLORE MORE
What consequences did this [living in Sodom] have for Lot (2 Peter 2:7-8)? Lot did not live at peace; he was tormented by what he saw and heard.

Read Genesis 19:1-8. Do you think Lot acted righteously? Lot's answer to the men of Sodom was not the most pious. He offered his two daughters to be raped. Never mind the customs of the time, which put a high value on the way you treated guests: this was not a godly answer.

11. What do you think Peter means by "follow[ing] the corrupt desires of the flesh" and "despis[ing] authority" (2 Peter 2:10)? (Look back at verses 1-3 to see some examples of how the false teachers were doing this.) Our sinful nature leads us to desire sin instead of righteousness. This constitutes rebellion against the authority of Jesus. In verses 1-3, we see the false teachers following their own desires by living in a depraved way (v 2) and acting with greed (v 3). We see them despising God's authority by denying him (v 1), bringing the way of truth into disrepute (v 2), and fabricating their own stories to replace his word (v 3).

12. APPLY: What particular teachings might tempt us to "despise [the] authority" of Jesus and Scripture today? Many teachings today question the word of God. People may tell us that the Bible is outdated, unreliable, or even immoral. Other teachings tempt us to change our understanding of God. This also leads us to despise his authority. For example, if we believe that God never comes in judgment, we will despise his commandments because we will not be afraid of the consequences of disobedience. Or if we believe that God wants to make us rich (as the prosperity gospel teaches), we will doubt and despise him when that doesn't happen. Another major issue today is the area of sexual ethics. Many want us to believe that God doesn't really mean what he says about this in the Bible. They may dismiss its teachings altogether or try to explain them away by saying they depend on context. It is tempting to go along with this, but in reality it is a rejection of God's authority. This link is clear in Romans 1:21-27. Encourage the group to think about specific times when they have been tempted to reject Jesus' authority and work out what false teaching may have lain behind that temptation.

- **Practically, how can we keep ourselves in the truth?** Peter tells us, "You will do well to pay attention" to God's inspired Scriptures (1:19). This is the best way of keeping ourselves in the truth. Ask group members to share specific practical ideas that have enabled them to keep on paying attention to God's word and helping others to do so.

3 2 Peter 2:10b-22
DON'T WANDER OFF

THE BIG IDEA
Sin might seem enticing, but that is a deception and it will be punished. If we know the truth, we must do all we can to stick to the right path.

SUMMARY
Peter previously warned us about the destruction that comes upon the ungodly. He now gives us an idea of how ungodly false teachers can be. He first describes their character. They are so arrogant that they curse celestial beings who are under God's judgment but whom even angels do not dare to curse (2:10-12). Peter compares them to irrational animals which are eventually captured and killed. In other words, God's judgment on them will be severe.

Next Peter describes their lifestyle, which is characterised by sin and which has a destructive impact on those around them (v 13-14). He compares them to Balaam, a prophet in Numbers 22 – 25 who was tempted to curse God's people in exchange for a bribe (2 Peter 2:15-16). Like him, they have "wandered off" from the path of righteousness.

They entice others to follow them with the promise of freedom, but they themselves are slaves of sin (v 18-20). Peter says that their actions have serious consequences. They have known the truth but have then chosen to live in violation of it (v 20-22). They have also sought to lead others astray. The result is that "blackest darkness is reserved for them" (v 17).

This passage is a warning. Once we have understood the truth and have been cleansed by Christ, we must not fall back into sin. Instead we must keep coming to him and following in his ways.

OPTIONAL EXTRA
Play the game "Two Truths and a Lie." Each person must say two true things about themselves and one lie. Everyone else has to guess which is which. This introduces the topic of truth and lies, which underpins today's study.

GUIDANCE FOR QUESTIONS
1. What's the link between the things we believe and the way we behave? Can you think of examples where someone's beliefs have led them to act in particular ways? This question is designed to make the link between the previous session—which focused on our knowledge of the truth—and this session, which is more about our lifestyles. We need to realise that the two are closely related! You could start the discussion by thinking about religious beliefs: how and why do adherents of different religions act differently? You could also talk about other kinds of belief. Examples could be as simple as believing it's going to rain and therefore wearing a coat.

2. Peter has said that the false teachers "despise authority." Why do they do that—what is their view of themselves (v 10)? They are "bold and arrogant."

- **But what is Peter's view of them (v 12)?** He considers them insolent, irrational, and arrogant. They are like animals which don't understand what

54 LEADER'S GUIDE | Standing firm

they're doing and which will eventually be captured and killed. In other words, God's judgment upon them will be severe.

3. What particular actions reveal their misguided arrogance (v 10-12)? They dared to curse "celestial beings" whose might was far superior to theirs. They thought that they had authority not only to judge these beings but also to speak abusively of them. But not even angels do this.

4. What lifestyle do the false teachers live (v 13-14)? They have no shame in displaying their immoral behavior. Their conscience is numb, so that they find immorality a pleasure. They are living this way even while they continue to meet with Christian brothers and sisters. They are guilty of adultery. They are not just sinful but characterized by sin—their desire for sin is insatiable. They "seduce the unstable": that is, rather than caring for the most vulnerable, they use them to satisfy their own appetites. Additionally, they are greedy. They are experts in how to take money from people.

- **What are they promising (v 18-19)? Why does this lifestyle seem attractive?** The false teachers invite people to live according to their own desires (v 18). They promise freedom (v 19). These are things all of us want!

5. What impact have they had...
- **on others (v 13, 14, 18)?**
  v 13: They have done harm; they are like blemishes on others' lives.
  v 14, 18: They seduce the unstable, taking advantage of the weakest believers to lead them astray. They "entice people who are just escaping from those who live in error." These are new converts who lack knowledge and are perhaps still struggling with recent sin in their lives. They are especially vulnerable to the temptation to go back to a sinful life.
- **on themselves (v 20)?** They are "entangled" and "overcome" by lies and sin. They have deceived themselves and ended up being controlled by sin.

6. APPLY: Who or what promises "freedom" today? What are they really offering people?
- Teachers of the prosperity gospel promise their disciples that they will be brought out of financial difficulty if they give such teachers money, because God will multiply their offering. But this promise is not biblical and only brings people into more financial problems.
- Many today teach "sexual freedom"—encouraging us to indulge any sexual desire we have. Again, this is not biblical and instead traps us.
- Some may desire to be free from belonging to a church community. They believe they can be Christians on their own. But without brothers and sisters alongside us, and without consistent, faithful Bible teaching, we easily stray into sin.
- You may be able to think of many more examples of your own. Make sure that at least some of the lies you discuss are relevant to your own cultural or church context.

EXPLORE MORE
Read Numbers 22:21-35. Why does the angel of the Lord stop Balaam? The angel of the Lord represents God. Balaam's way is "perverse" (v 32, ESV) to God. In other words, he is doing the wrong thing.

What's the contrast between Balaam

and the donkey? The donkey is more virtuous than Balaam! It heeds God's warning, but Balaam is blind to it.

In 2 Peter 2:15, how does Peter highlight Balaam's sinfulness? He describes it as "madness." Even Balaam's donkey knew that he was doing wrong!

7. Peter says that the false teachers "left the straight way and wandered off" (v 15). In verses 20-21, how else does he describe what has happened? They have escaped the corruption of the world by knowing Jesus, but then they have become entangled in it again. They have known the way of righteousness, and then turned their backs on it.

- **Verse 22 compares the false teachers to a dog returning to its vomit and a sow returning to the mud. What have the false teachers returned to?** They have returned to the sinful lives they lived before they first heard the message about God.

8. Why is what they have done so serious (v 20-21)? Knowing the truth only to live in violation of it is worse than living in ignorance of it. They know about Jesus, but they have turned their back on him. They are trampling over Jesus' blood and behaving like pagans, but under the name of Jesus. This brings terrible consequences.

9. How do you think this happened? What might the first steps have been? We know that the false teachers were greedy and adulterous (v 14). Perhaps it was money or lust that first tempted them away from the right path. For all of us there will be some particular pleasure which tempts us away from what is right. Once we have fallen into temptation, we begin to rationalize our sin, and this leads us into false doctrines.

10. What's the end result of taking this path? Look back through the passage and find all the times Peter highlights the false teachers' ultimate destiny. These false teachers will come under God's judgment and be destroyed. Peter states this in verses 1, 3, 9-10, 12, 13, and 17.

11. Look back at 2 Peter 1. What does Peter want his readers to do, in order to avoid becoming like the false teachers? We should remember the truth we have been taught (1:15) and make every effort to live godly lives (v 5-8).

12. APPLY: When we are tempted to sin, what should we do? We must look to Jesus. Remembering his truth will keep us from sinning. The power of his Spirit within us will also help us. Even when we do fall, we can keep on coming to Christ. The author of Hebrews tells us, "Encourage one another daily, as long as it is called 'Today,' so that none of you may be hardened by sin's deceitfulness" (Hebrews 3:13). When we are tempted, we should ask others in the body of Christ for help. We could ask someone to pray, or to advise us, or to simply keep encouraging us to obey in this particular area. In Christ there is an opportunity every day—even every hour—to return to his ways and be cleansed and forgiven once again. But we must also remind ourselves of what the alternative is: the destruction that lies behind the sin that falsely promises freedom.

4

2 Peter 3:1-18

HOW TO WAIT FOR THE SECOND COMING

THE BIG IDEA

The day of judgment gives us two reasons to live godly lives: the wicked will be destroyed, and there will be a new world full of righteousness.

SUMMARY

After warning us about the immorality of false teachers, Peter now shifts his focus to contradicting a specific teaching which had been introduced into the church. The false teachers were denying the possibility of Christ's return. The apostle knows that if someone can be convinced that Christ will not return to judge the world, it will be easy to convince them to live sinfully. So he reminds them of the truth of the second coming in order to "stimulate [them] to wholesome thinking" (3:1).

Scoffers argue that judgment has not yet happened, and so it never will, but Peter affirms that God has come in judgment before, and so he will again (v 3-7). He gives two reasons to explain why our Lord has not yet returned (v 8-9). First, God does not count time as we do, so he is not really delaying. Second, God is patient. He is waiting for more people to come to repentance before he comes in judgment.

What will that day be like? Peter describes it in verse 10: it will happen suddenly, and everything will be destroyed. Sin has had such a devastating effect on God's creation that everything will have to be consumed. (There are two interpretations of what it means that creation will be destroyed and that there will be a new heaven and a new earth. Some argue that everything will be destroyed and there will be an entirely new creation, while others prefer to speak of the renewal of the fallen creation. Whichever, it is certainly clear that there will be destruction, and there will be something new.) Therefore, Peter calls us to live godly lives (v 11-14). He highlights two closely related motivations. First, we are to avoid sin because we take seriously the threat of judgment. Second, we are to live righteously because this is consistent with the new world that is coming.

Peter speaks once again about seeing the Lord's delay as a sign of patience, but he acknowledges that some distort this doctrine (v 15-16). We can see what this distortion was in Paul's letters: some were saying that it doesn't matter how much someone sins, since God will always forgive them. But Peter tells us to guard a true understanding of God's patience and of how we should live (v 17). He calls us to grow in the grace and knowledge of the Lord. This means growing in knowledge of God's character and becoming more like him. Our call is to live a holy and godly life, and to be devoted to God.

OPTIONAL EXTRA

Here is a charades-type game to introduce the idea of Jesus' return. Put the group into pairs and give each pair a scenario in which one person returns and is greeted by the other. The rest of the group has to guess what relationship the two people have and how long they have been apart. For example: a child greeting a parent at the end of a school day; someone meeting a long-lost sibling; an estranged husband and wife meeting unexpectedly; an employee greeting his boss as she returns to a meeting after a brief phone call. Or make up your own scenarios!

GUIDANCE FOR QUESTIONS

1. What is your understanding of what will happen when Jesus returns? In many circles, the second coming of Christ is not a frequent topic of conversation these days. So before you read this chapter of 2 Peter, which is all about looking forward to that day, it will be helpful to find out what assumptions people already have.

2. Peter starts by reminding us of the purpose of his letter. What does he want his readers to do (v 1-2)? Peter calls his disciples to remember. They should think in a sober manner and have a clear understanding about the truths that have been revealed to them. Their thinking must remain "wholesome": clear, logical, consistent, and morally pure.

3. He specifically wants us to believe in the second coming of the Lord Jesus. What does he say will happen on that day (v 7)? All of creation will be consumed by fire. This will be a day of judgment for the destruction of the ungodly.

4. Some people say this won't happen. Why (v 3-4)? False teachers scoff at the doctrine of the second coming. This is because they live to please the flesh—following their evil desires (v 3). They don't want to believe that their sin will be judged. The fulfilment of God's promise has not come yet, so they affirm that it will never be fulfilled (v 4). Nothing has changed since the beginning of creation, so, they presume, it never will.

5. Peter reminds us of the flood in order to counter the false teachers' argument (v 5-7). Why? What connections are there between the flood and the second coming? God flooded the whole world in judgment because humanity was so corrupt. The next judgment will take place for the same reason and "by the same word" (v 7). It will be even greater—both the heavens and the earth will be subject to destruction.

6. How does Peter explain why God seems to be slow in keeping his promise (v 8-9)? First, the Lord lives outside of time and space, so he does not count time as we do (v 8). Christ ascended to his throne 2,000 years ago, but in God's calendar, it is as if Christ left today. God is not delayed—not according to how he measures time. He is "not slow" (v 9). Second, God is patient (v 9). He could carry out his judgment right now, but he has not done so because there are people who will come to salvation today, tomorrow, next month, and beyond. Desiring that they all come to repentance, he has delayed his judgment in our favor. What detains the Lord's judgment, in other words, is not our good behavior but his infinite goodness.

7. APPLY: If we are looking forward to the second coming of Jesus, what should our attitude be now toward wickedness and ungodly people? Knowing that there are consequences for acting unjustly, we will be motivated to live morally and not to go along with wickedness. This will also help us to be patient when the wicked prosper; we know that complete justice is coming. The second coming should also motivate us to share the good news of Jesus with those around us, even those who seem least likely to accept it. Perhaps they may be one of those whom the Lord wants to come to repentance.

8. What will the day of the Lord be like (v 10)?
- It will come like a thief: suddenly and by surprise.
- Everyone will know when it comes, because the heavens will disappear "with a roar."
- The earth will be laid bare and the elements will be destroyed. Sin has had such a devastating effect on God's creation that everything will have to be consumed and removed.

9. How should this motivate us to live (v 11-14)?
We should live in a godly manner (v 11), looking forward to the second coming (v 12) and to the new world it will bring (v 13). We should "make every effort to be found spotless, blameless, and at peace with him" (v 14).

- **Why?** First, we are to avoid sin because as we look forward to the second coming, we take seriously the threat of judgment. This day of accountability is for everyone—which calls for sobriety. If we have accepted Christ's spotless sacrifice on our behalf, then we are at peace with him, and we should live in the light of that. Second, we are to live lives that are righteous in order to reflect the new order that will be inaugurated with the coming of the Lord: a new world in which righteousness will reign.

10. What does Peter think about this interpretation of Paul's teaching (v 16)?
It is a distortion—not only of Paul's teaching but of the rest of Scripture. Peter calls such teachers "ignorant and unstable." They are heading for destruction.

- **How do you think Peter would counter their argument? (Look back at 1:19-21; 2:4-10; and 3:5-7.)**
  - Scripture must not be distorted because it is completely reliable and comes from God (1:19-21). What it says about the second coming must be true.
  - Peter has already cited several examples of God's judgments in the past (2:4-10, 3:5-7). It is clear that God punishes the unjust.

EXPLORE MORE
Read Romans 6:1-2. Why are some people saying we should keep on sinning (v 1)? So that grace will increase. The argument is that if we sin more, we will gain more forgiveness.

But why does this make no sense (v 2)? Paul says we have become new people. We have died to sin. Sin no longer masters us. So why would we live sinfully?

Read Romans 6:22-23. How do we gain eternal life? Eternal life is a gift from God. We gain this gift by accepting Jesus as our Lord. This makes us "slaves of God," which means we will live righteously.

How could we use Paul's words to answer someone who says, "If you're forgiven, you can just sin as much as you want"? Continuing to sin makes no sense! How can we who died to sin still live in it (v 2)? We should embrace the new and eternal life God has given us (v 22). Given how much Jesus has done for us in setting us free from sin, this is the only appropriate response.

11. APPLY: Why is it so important to "be on your guard" (v 17) about

what you believe about the second coming in particular? It is easy to fall into the errors of the false teachers and stop believing that the second coming will ever really happen. It seems so far off and so unlikely, humanly speaking. This is why it is so important to guard our understanding about this doctrine in particular. Knowing about the second coming helps us to have the right perspective on our lives, and therefore enables us to live in a godly way. Looking forward to the day of judgment motivates us to reject sin and pursue righteousness. It helps us to prioritize the things of God rather than becoming too comfortable in this world. It gives us the right understanding of God as both merciful and just.

12: APPLY: Peter calls us to grow in grace (which means growing to be like Jesus) and in the knowledge of God (v 18). How can you seek this kind of growth this week? Some may want to be more disciplined in their prayer life or read the Bible more regularly. Some may decide to pursue some theological education or read more Christian books, so as to understand Christian doctrine better. Some may talk about becoming more closely involved with church or seeking to serve others more. Your group may also be willing to discuss specific areas in which they wish to grow. Perhaps there are particular sins which they need help to fight against, or particular situations where they are finding it hard to be godly.

5 Jude v 1-11
FIGHT FOR THE FAITH

THE BIG IDEA
God has given us faith; now we must fight to uphold it. This means acknowledging God's authority in every area of our lives.

SUMMARY
Jude introduces himself as a servant of Jesus and brother of James—probably James the brother of Jesus. So Jude was probably Jesus' brother (or half-brother) too (see Matthew 13:55; Mark 6:3). He opens his letter by describing his readers as those who have been called, loved by God and kept for Jesus Christ (v 1), and wishing them blessings from God (v 2). It is God who guarantees our final destiny and keeps hold of us. Yet in verse 3 Jude urges us to "contend for the faith." He wants us to maintain the purity of the faith—not adding to or altering the gospel message in any way. But he also wants us to defend the implications of what we believe—living moral lives in the light of what Jesus has done for us. This becomes clear as Jude describes the moral and doctrinal corruption of false teachers who have "slipped in" among his readers (v 4). He does not want us to follow in their footsteps.

In verses 5-7 Jude uses three stories from the Old Testament to remind us that, although God is loving and slow to anger, he is not without anger. He does not leave the guilty unpunished. There is no way for these false teachers to escape God's judgment. Jude mentions the Israelites who were destroyed in the desert because they did not believe (v 5; see Numbers 14:1-38); angels who rebelled against God (v 6; this may be a reference to Genesis 6:2); and the people of Sodom and Gomorrah, who were destroyed because they pursued sexual immorality (v 7; see Genesis 18:20 – 19:29).

Jude seeks to show us that the false teachers of his own time are every bit as deserving of punishment (v 8-10). They act immorally and reject God's authority. He contrasts them with the archangel Michael, who submitted to God's authority and therefore did not dare to pronounce judgment against the devil. Unlike him, the false teachers "heap abuse on celestial beings." This will result in their destruction.

(This story comes from a book that is not part of Scripture, but which the primitive church knew and believed. Jude, under the inspiration of the Spirit, reached outside Scripture to add details which we would not otherwise have been sure about. This doesn't mean that we should accept everything in the book he is referring to: we can trust that the books we have in the Bible are the ones inspired by God, and no others.)

Finally, Jude compares the false teachers with three biblical characters who serve as further examples of sin that has been judged by God: Cain, Balaam, and Korah (v 11; see Genesis 4:1-16; Numbers 22; Numbers 16:1-35).

OPTIONAL EXTRA
Find some examples of famous people who "fight" in some way, and ask the group to say what they fight for and how. Start with obvious ones: for example, Muhammad Ali was a professional fighter! Include those who fight for particular causes, such as

Greta Thunberg, and those who have fought high-profile court cases, such as the accusers of Harvey Weinstein. Include an athlete such as the sprinter Usain Bolt or the gymnast Simone Biles, who "fight" to win a prize. They could be people you admire or people you don't!

GUIDANCE FOR QUESTIONS

1. "It's worth fighting for." What might we say that about? You may discuss loved ones, moral principles, or other causes. Encourage group members to share specifically what they are ready to fight for.

2. What three privileges of Christians does Jude highlight in verse 1? We are "called": specifically chosen by God, not because of anything we have done but because of his Son. We are also "loved in God the Father." Finally, we are "kept for Jesus Christ." The Father is preserving us to honor and glorify his Son for the rest of eternity.

- **What three blessings does he pray for his readers in verse 2?** Mercy, peace, and love.

3. Why does Jude feel "compelled" to write (v 3)? What has happened? Originally, Jude wanted to encourage his readers about salvation. But he felt "compelled" to change his initial intention and instead speak about the need to defend the faith. This is because false teachers have "slipped in" among the believers.

Jude's opponents "pervert[ed] the grace of our God into a license for immorality." In other words, they claimed that believers could live as they wished, counting on God's grace to forgive them in the future. But God did not give us his grace to encourage us to sin freely; he gave it to empower us to obey all of his commandments.

4. Jude wants his readers to "contend" (or fight) for the faith.

- **Why do you think it is important that this faith has been entrusted to them "once for all" (v 3)?** This vital phrase makes us aware that there is no place for new doctrinal teaching. We have already received the completed revelation that we need.

- **Why do you think Jude describes faith as something to be fought for?** Jude is saying that we must struggle to defend the faith against false additions and re-interpretations. False teachers will continually plague us, so we must be on our guard to make sure the gospel is not altered in any way. But "faith" does not just mean our belief in Christ but also our obedience to him. Obedience is difficult because we are fallen and sinful. So we must also fight against sin.

5. Taking into account both verse 1 and verses 3-4, what does it mean to have faith in Jesus? Faith starts with God loving us and choosing us (v 1). It is given to us by the grace of God (v 4). It involves trusting Jesus as "our only Sovereign and Lord" (v 4). But it also involves effort: we are to live obedient, moral lives (unlike the false teachers, v 4). Our faith involves truths which have been entrusted to us once and for all (v 3), which must not be changed or compromised.

6. APPLY: What does it look like to uphold Jesus as "our only Sovereign and Lord" (v 3)? We should embrace the whole will of God, obeying everything he has commanded us. This means living moral lives because we recognize Jesus' authority over everything we do. Encourage the group to talk through different scenarios or areas of life. What does it mean for Jesus to be Lord when we are at work, at home, at church, or with non-Christian friends?

7. In the examples in verses 5-7, what did God do, and why? You may wish to get your group to look back at the Old Testament narratives of these stories. Suggest that the group splits in two: one should read Numbers 14:1-38 and the other Genesis 18:20 – 19:29. The example of the angels in verse 6 is probably a reference to Genesis 6:2, but we are not given the entire narrative in Scripture.

- **v 5:** God, in his mercy, took his people out of Egypt. But he also destroyed those who did not believe while they were in the desert (see Numbers 13 – 14).
- **v 6:** Certain angels rejected the place God had given them. So he has imprisoned them ready for the day of judgment. We have already seen a reference to these angels in 2 Peter 2:4.
- **v 7:** God destroyed Sodom and Gomorrah with fire because the inhabitants of these towns "gave themselves up" to sexual immorality. This is described in Genesis 18 – 19.
- **Why do you think Jude wants to remind his readers of these things?** All these sins met with judgment. We can be sure that those who pursue sin in any age will meet with judgment too.

8. What are the "ungodly people" of Jude's day doing, and on what basis (v 8)? These false teachers are polluting their bodies—this probably refers to sexual immorality. They have rejected God's authority and heaped abuse on celestial beings. In other words, they presume to have great power and authority, which they think enables them to speak against angelic beings. We saw a similar idea in 2 Peter 2:10-12. The false teachers base their behavior on dreams instead of on the revealed word of God.

EXPLORE MORE
How does this [Michael's actions] show respect for God's authority? Michael left the judgment to God instead of pronouncing judgment by his own authority.
Read Revelation 12:7-10. How is God's authority made clear here? God is far more powerful than Satan. Satan is defeated and hurled down immediately (v 8). Then a voice says that the kingdom of God and the authority of the Messiah have come (v 10). Satan's power, such as it was, is broken.

9. How do these examples match what the false teachers of Jude's own day are doing? Think especially about...
- **their attitude toward God's authority:** They reject God's authority and act on their own understanding of what is right instead (v 8). This is like Cain, who made an offering which God rejected, and then became angry that God had not done what he wanted. Similarly, they have rebelled against God's revealed word, like Korah, who rebelled against God's appointed prophets.
- **their motivation:** Like Balaam, they are motivated by greed, acting "for profit" (v 11).
- **their final destiny:** All the people in Jude's examples met with death as a result of their sin. Likewise, he tells us that the false teachers are destined for destruction (v 4, 10). In fact, he tells us they have already "been destroyed" (v 11).

10. What do all Jude's examples tell us about how and why people might fall into sin? All these examples show us paths to rebellion against God.
- The Israelites in the wilderness disbelieved God's promise because they were afraid and intimidated. Fear led them into sin, because they thought that God was not powerful and that his plans for them were not good.
- The angels who rebelled against God simply wanted more. They were not satisfied with the place he had given them. This attitude can lead us, too, into sin.
- The example of Sodom and Gomorrah reminds us of how tempting sexual immorality can be.
- Cain set his own standards instead of seeking to do what God wanted. This was another way of rebelling against God's authority. When confronted with his sin, he became angry instead of repenting. He continued in his rebellion and murdered his brother. We must make sure that if someone confronts us about our sin, we have a humble and teachable attitude!
- The story of Balaam highlights how easily we succumb to the seductive power of money.
- Korah rebelled against the authority of God's appointed leaders. God continues to establish patterns of authority: citizens to governments, wives to husbands, children to parents, staff to employers, and believers to pastors and elders (see Ephesians 5:21 – 6:9; 1 Peter 2:11 – 3:7). When we violate these lines of authority, we are on a path toward rebelling against God himself.

11. Based on what we have read so far, how would you sum up…
- **what it means to sin?** Sin is rebellion against God.
- **God's attitude toward sin?** God is extremely angry with those who corrupt his design and violate his law.
- **what attitude we ought to have toward God?** We must accept him as "our only Sovereign and Lord" (v 3).

12. APPLY: Imagine you realized that a fellow believer was being tempted toward sin. How could you follow Jude's example and help them to contend for their faith? Jude's concern for his readers is plain. He addresses them as "dear friends" (v 3) and shows his heart by wishing them blessings from God (v 2). But he is not afraid to use very strong language as he warns them about the dangers of immorality. However, he does not write in an accusatory way. He goes to Scripture and reminds them of truths they know about God. We can follow his example in all these things as we seek to encourage and strengthen our brothers and sisters in Christ.

6 Jude v 12-25
GLORIOUS MERCY

THE BIG IDEA
While those who pursue ungodliness are on a path to death, there is great hope for repentant sinners. We can contend for the faith together—and know that we have God's help too.

SUMMARY
Jude wants his readers to understand at a deeper level how evil the false teachers are. So he describes them using six metaphors which highlight their immoral character, their negative impact on believers, and the punishment that awaits them (v 12-13). Next, he cites a prophecy from the book of Enoch which foretells the destruction of the ungodly (v 14-15; Enoch is not part of inspired Scripture, but Jude does want us to listen to these words). He also cites the apostles' teaching, which predicted the existence of these ungodly teachers (v 17-18).

In verses 16 and 19 Jude tells us some of the specific sins of the false teachers. His language so far has been very severe. But at the same time he is very sensitive and tender toward the believers. He is motivated by love and wants to call them to a higher standard of living.

So, he seeks to leave a word of instruction regarding how to contend for the faith (v 20-23). He encourages us to build ourselves up, praying in the Spirit and keeping ourselves in God's love. We are to persevere as we wait for the second coming. This involves obeying God's commandments and asking for the Spirit's help to do God's will. He also tells us what to do with those who do not have the same degree of faithfulness. We are to have mercy on them and make every effort to call them back to the right path.

The final verses turn to the glory of the Creator God (v 24-25). He is the one who guarantees our salvation and keeps us from stumbling. He is also the one to whom all glory, majesty, power, and authority are due. These are words of praise to the only God of the entire universe.

OPTIONAL EXTRA
Run a team-building game that will help your group explore the fact that we need help from God and one another to make it to the finish line of faith. Set up a simple obstacle course with plastic cups laid out on the floor. Put the group into teams. One person in each team is blindfolded and must make it from one side of the course to the other without stepping on any cups. The rest of the team must give them directions. You could also try a variation in which other team members are allowed to hold the blindfolded person's hand and push and pull them gently to help them know where to go.

GUIDANCE FOR QUESTIONS
1. When you see someone doing something wrong, what do you tend to do? Some may ignore it or pretend they haven't seen it. Some may immediately rebuke the person. Some may take a step back and consider the situation before interfering more gently. Of course, it will

depend on the specific situation! This question is designed to get the group warmed up and thinking about how we can follow in Jude's footsteps and contend for others' faith as well as our own.

2. What do the images in verses 12-13 show about...
- **the false teachers' impact on Jude's readers?**
  - The word "blemishes" (v 12) can also be translated "hidden reefs" (ESV)—showing that they are shipwrecking people's lives.
  - The false teachers should be "shepherds"—this probably means they had positions of authority, perhaps as pastors—but they use their flock for personal benefit instead of caring for the sheep.
  - They are empty clouds. Palestine has always been an arid place. Imagine living in that region and watching clouds come your way; yet when they arrive, they do not rain! These false teachers promise a lot, but they have no life-bringing water to give their followers.
- **their character?**
  - They are selfish and greedy—"shepherds who feed only themselves" (v 12).
  - The comparison to "wild waves" (v 13) suggests that they make a lot of noise, but that this does not produce any effect. They just foam up shame because what they do is immoral.
- **their ultimate destiny?** Like an uprooted tree, it is already as if they were dead (v 12). Like shooting stars, they will be quickly destroyed (v 13).

3. What did Enoch say would happen to "ungodly sinners"? God will come to judge and convict them of their sin.

4. What specific examples of the false teachers' sin does Jude list in verse 16?
- They are grumblers and faultfinders. When we complain, our grumbling is not really against people but against God. We are finding fault with the situations that he has put us in or the people he has placed in our paths.
- They follow their own evil desires. This implies that they satisfy their lusts.
- They boast about themselves. This is a far cry from the gentle and humble character of Jesus.
- They flatter others in order to get their own way. In other words, they are self-centered and concerned only about their own interests and gains.

5. How does Jude help us to understand why these people are acting the way they do (v 17-19)? They are simply following their own desires (v 18). This is a natural human instinct (v 19): naturally, we all want our own way! The false teachers "do not have the Spirit" (Jude 19). But when we have the Holy Spirit, we are able to say "Jesus is Lord" (1 Corinthians 12:3), which means we submit to his authority instead of our own.

6. Jude's condemnation of sin is very severe. But how does he show tenderness as he addresses his readers? In verses 17 and 20, he calls his readers "dear friends." These words were also used in verse 3.

- **What does he call them to do (v 20)?** Jude's first word of instruction regarding how to contend for the faith tells us to build ourselves up in our faith. This is a call to grow in our faith both as individuals and within the Christian community—the NLT translates this phrase "build each other up." He also calls us to pray in the

Spirit. Although the Bible does not give us detailed instruction on how to pray in the Spirit, it is clear that the Spirit does help us in even our wordless prayers (Romans 8:26). We should pray in accordance with the word of God, so that our petitions and hopes align with God's revealed will (Romans 8:27). We pray that God's will may be done on earth (Matthew 6:10).

7. APPLY: How does this give us hope in our own struggles with sin? The way Jude addresses his readers is entirely different from the way he describes the false teachers. Jude is confident of his readers' salvation; the false teachers do not have the Spirit, but he encourages his readers to pray in the Spirit. We, too, can be confident that if we call on the name of Jesus, we will be given the help we need, and we will be brought to eternal life (v 21).

- **What can we do practically to put Jude's instructions into practice?**
  - Listen to the word. God gave his church pastors and teachers specifically in order to build up the body of Christ (Ephesians 4:11-13). We should listen to our teachers and obey their instruction.
  - Pray. We can pray for God's will to be done. We can ask God to place in us the desire to do the things to which he is calling us, and to give us the ability to carry them out. We can also ask the Spirit to intercede for us when we do not know what to pray (Romans 8:26).
  - Obey God's commandments (see Explore More, below).

EXPLORE MORE
Read John 15:10 and 1 John 3:24. What does it mean to keep ourselves in God's love? The way we remain in God's love is by obeying his commandments.

8. In verses 22-23, how does Jude call us to show the same tenderness toward fellow believers and the same hatred of sin that he has shown? Jude outlines three types of straying believers here. First, he calls us to have mercy on those who doubt. Second, the word "snatching" (v 23) suggests that we are to do everything within our power to get those who are falling into sin to return to the faith. This demonstrates Jude's deep concern for his fellow believers. At the same time, he tells us to hate "even the clothing stained by corrupted flesh". Third, with some people, Jude wants us to be careful that we ourselves do not fall into their sin. He is determined to help us avoid sin.

9. APPLY: How can we put these instructions into practice—contending for one another's faith as well as our own? We should spare no effort as we seek to build one another up in faith. We should be on the lookout for those who are doubting or in danger of falling into sin. We should even make efforts to restore those who are living in sin. All of this involves tenderness and love as well as serious warnings. We must also be careful to protect our own lives and cultivate holiness. All of us are at risk of falling into immorality. Encourage your group to discuss these things as practically as possible—though without getting too personal, as this may not be appropriate in a group context.

10. What is God able to do for us (v 24)? He guarantees our salvation. The Holy Spirit dwells inside us in order to keep us from losing our salvation. We may still sin—though we also have the Spirit's help to keep us from sinning—but once we have been saved, we are "kept" (v 1) and will one day be presented before God's presence.

Having been cleansed by Christ's blood, we will come into his presence with joy, rather than with trembling and fear.

11. What do we owe him (v 25)? We should acknowledge God's glory: the fact that everything in the universe revolves around him, and that he is the author of it all. We should acknowledge his majesty—his greatness and splendor—and his power and authority. This is the God we honor.

12. APPLY: How will recognizing these things keep us from stumbling? If we realise how powerful and how wonderful God is, we will want to honor him with all our words and deeds. If we make him Lord of our life, he will keep us from falling.

- **What can we do to keep reminding ourselves of these truths?** Encourage the group to pool ideas: what reminds each of them of these truths? This question could link with the PRAY section.

Expository Guide to 2 Peter and Jude by Miguel Núñez

This expository guide by Miguel Núñez unpacks these two short letters verse by verse, showing how they are still utterly relevant to us today. This unique resource can be can be used for personal devotions, or used by small group leaders and preachers to help them teach Scripture to others.

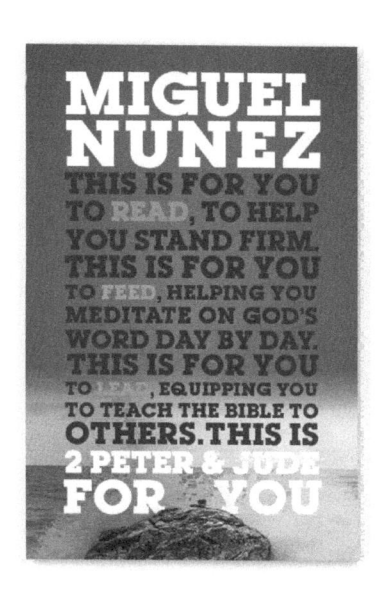

Explore our whole range of expository guides

thegoodbook.com/for-you
thegoodbook.co.uk/for-you
thegoodbook.com.au/for-you

Good Book Guides | The full range

OLD TESTAMENT

Exodus: 8 Studies
Tim Chester
ISBN: 9781784980269

Judges: 6 Studies
Timothy Keller
ISBN: 9781908762887

Ruth: 4 Studies
Tim Chester
ISBN: 9781905564910

Ruth: 7 Studies
Tony Merida
ISBN: 9781784983888

David: 6 Studies
Nathan Buttery
ISBN: 9781904889984

1 Samuel: 6 Studies
Tim Chester
ISBN: 9781909919594

2 Samuel: 6 Studies
Tim Chester
ISBN: 9781784982195

1 Kings 1–11: 8 Studies
James Hughes
ISBN: 9781907377976

Esther: 7 Studies
Jane McNabb
ISBN: 9781908317926

Nehemiah: 8 Studies
Eric Mason
ISBN: 9781784986773

Psalms: 6 Studies
Tim Chester
ISBN: 9781904889960

Psalms: 7 Studies
Christopher Ash &
Alison Mitchell
ISBN: 9781904889960

Proverbs: 8 Studies
Kathleen Nielson & Rachel Jones
ISBN: 9781784984304

Ezekiel: 6 Studies
Tim Chester
ISBN: 9781904889274

Daniel: 7 Studies
David Helm
ISBN: 9781910307328

Hosea: 8 Studies
Dan Wells
ISBN: 9781905564255

Jonah: 6 Studies
Stephen Witmer
ISBN: 9781907377433

Micah: 6 Studies
Stephen Um
ISBN: 9781909559738

Zechariah: 6 Studies
Tim Chester
ISBN: 9781904889267

NEW TESTAMENT

Mark: 10 Studies
Jason Meyer
ISBN: 9781784983031

Mark 1–8: 10 Studies
Tim Chester
ISBN: 9781904889281

Mark 9–16: 7 Studies
Tim Chester
ISBN: 9781904889519

Luke 1–12: 8 Studies
Mike McKinley
ISBN: 9781784980160

Luke 12–24: 8 Studies
Mike McKinley
ISBN: 9781784981174

John 1–12: 8 Studies
Josh Moody
ISBN: 9781784982188

John 13–21: 8 Studies
Josh Moody
ISBN: 9781784983611

Acts 1–12: 8 Studies
R. Albert Mohler, Jr.
ISBN: 9781910307007

Acts 13–28: 8 Studies
R. Albert Mohler, Jr.
ISBN: 9781910307014

Romans 1–7: 7 Studies
Timothy Keller
ISBN: 9781908762924

Romans 8–16: 7 Studies
Timothy Keller
ISBN: 9781910307311

1 Corinthians 1–9: 7 Studies
Mark Dever
ISBN: 9781908317681

1 Corinthians 10–16: 8 Studies
Mark Dever & Carl Laferton
ISBN: 9781908317964

1 Corinthians: 8 Studies
Andrew Wilson
ISBN: 9781784986254

2 Corinthians: 7 Studies
Gary Millar
ISBN: 9781784983895

Galatians: 7 Studies
Timothy Keller
ISBN: 9781908762566

Ephesians: 10 Studies
Thabiti Anyabwile
ISBN: 9781907377099

Ephesians: 8 Studies
Richard Coekin
ISBN: 9781910307694

Philippians: 7 Studies
Steven J. Lawson
ISBN: 9781784981181

Colossians: 6 Studies
Mark Meynell
ISBN: 9781906334246

1 & 2 Thessalonians: 8 Studies
Ligon Duncan
ISBN: 9781784985011

1 & 2 Timothy: 7 Studies
Phillip Jensen
ISBN: 9781784980191

Titus: 5 Studies
Tim Chester
ISBN: 9781909919631

Hebrews: 8 Studies
Michael J. Kruger
ISBN: 9781784986049

James: 6 Studies
Sam Allberry
ISBN: 9781910307816

1 Peter: 6 Studies
Juan R. Sanchez
ISBN: 9781784980177

2 Peter & Jude: 6 Studies
Miguel Núñez
ISBN: 9781784987121

1 John: 7 Studies
Nathan Buttery
ISBN: 9781904889953

Revelation: 7 Studies
Tim Chester
ISBN: 9781910307021

TOPICAL

Man of God: 10 Studies
Anthony Bewes & Sam Allberry
ISBN: 9781904889977

Biblical Womanhood: 10 Studies
Sarah Collins
ISBN: 9781907377532

The Apostles' Creed: 10 Studies
Tim Chester
ISBN: 9781905564415

Promises Kept Bible Overview: 9 Studies
Carl Laferton
ISBN: 9781908317933

Contentment: 6 Studies
Anne Woodcock
ISBN: 9781905564668

The Reformation Solas: 6 Studies
Jason Helopoulos
ISBN: 9781784981501

Women of Faith: 8 Studies
Mary Davis
ISBN: 9781904889526

Introducing Jesus: 7 Studies
Tim Chester
ISBN: 9781907377129

Meeting Jesus: 8 Studies
Jenna Kavonic
ISBN: 9781905564460

Heaven: 6 Studies
Andy Telfer
ISBN: 9781909919457

Mission: 7 Studies
Alan Purser
ISBN: 9781784983628

Making Work Work: 8 Studies
Marcus Nodder
ISBN: 9781908762894

The Holy Spirit: 8 Studies
Pete & Anne Woodcock
ISBN: 9781905564217

Experiencing God: 6 Studies
Tim Chester
ISBN: 9781906334437

Real Prayer: 7 Studies
Anne Woodcock
ISBN: 9781910307595

Soul Songs: 6 Studies
Tim Chester
ISBN: 9781904889960

Mission: 7 Studies
Alan Purser
ISBN: 9781784983628

The Lord's Prayer: 7 Studies
Tim Chester
ISBN: 9781784985202

Church: 8 Studies
Anne Woodcock
ISBN: 9781784984199

Explore the whole range of Good Book Guides

thegoodbook.com/gbgs
thegoodbook.co.uk/gbgs
thegoodbook.com.au/gbgs

The God's Word For You Series

- **Exodus For You**
  Tim Chester
- **Judges For You**
  Timothy Keller
- **Ruth For You**
  Tony Merida
- **1 Samuel For You**
  Tim Chester
- **2 Samuel For You**
  Tim Chester
- **Nehemiah For You**
  Eric Mason
- **Psalms For You**
  Christopher Ash
- **Proverbs For You**
  Kathleen Nielson
- **Isaiah For You**
  Tim Chester
- **Daniel For You**
  David Helm
- **Mark For You**
  Jason Meyer
- **Luke 1-12 For You**
  Mike McKinley
- **Luke 12-24 For You**
  Mike McKinley
- **John 1-12 For You**
  Josh Moody
- **John 13-21 For You**
  Josh Moody
- **Acts 1-12 For You**
  Albert Mohler
- **Acts 13-28 For You**
  Albert Mohler

- **Romans 1-7 For You**
  Timothy Keller
- **Romans 8-16 For You**
  Timothy Keller
- **1 Corinthians For You**
  Andrew Wilson
- **2 Corinthians For You**
  Gary Millar
- **Galatians For You**
  Timothy Keller
- **Ephesians For You**
  Richard Coekin
- **Philippians For You**
  Steven Lawson
- **Colossians & Philemon For You**
  Mark Meynell
- **1 & 2 Thessalonians For You**
  Ligon Duncan
- **1 & 2 Timothy For You**
  Phillip Jensen
- **Titus For You**
  Tim Chester
- **Hebrews For You**
  Michael J. Kruger
- **James For You**
  Sam Allberry
- **1 Peter For You**
  Juan Sanchez
- **2 Peter & Jude For You**
  Miguel Nunez
- **Revelation For You**
  Tim Chester

For the full range, go to

thegoodbook.com/for-you
thegoodbook.co.uk/for-you
thegoodbook.com.au/for-you

Explore Daily Devotional

Explore Bible devotions help you to open the Scriptures every day and will encourage you in your Christian walk. Available as a booklet or as an app, Explore devotions are written by trusted Bible teachers, including Sam Allberry, Tim Chester, Christopher Ash, and many others who have written books in the God's Word For You series.

thegoodbook.com/devotionals/explore
thegoodbook.co.uk/daily-bible-reading/explore
thegoodbook.com.au/daily-bible-reading/explore

Join the *explore* community

The *Explore* Facebook group is a community of people who use *Explore* to study the Bible each day.

This is the place to share your thoughts, questions, encouragements, and prayers as you read *Explore*, and interact with other readers, as well as contributors, from around the world. No questions are too simple or too difficult to ask.

JOIN NOW:
facebook.com/groups/tgbc.explore

thegoodbook
COMPANY

BIBLICAL | RELEVANT | ACCESSIBLE

At The Good Book Company we are dedicated to helping Christians and local churches grow. We believe that God's growth process always starts with hearing clearly what he has said to us through his timeless and flawless word—the Bible.

Ever since we opened our doors in 1991, we have been striving to produce resources that are biblical, relevant, and accessible. By God's grace, we have grown to become an international publisher, encouraging ordinary Christians of every age and stage and every background and denomination to live for Christ day by day and equipping churches to grow in their knowledge of God, their love for one another, and the effectiveness of their outreach.

Call one of our friendly team for a discussion of your needs or visit one of our local websites for more information on the resources and services we provide.

Your friends at The Good Book Company

thegoodbook.com | thegoodbook.co.uk
thegoodbook.com.au | thegoodbook.co.nz
thegoodbook.co.in